Renewed Horizons: Embracing Life After Rehab

Kaitlyn Doht

Published by Kaitlyn Doht, 2024.

RENEWED HORIZONS: EMBRACING LIFE AFTER REHAB

First edition. October 24, 2024.

ISBN: 979-8227065667

Written by Kaitlyn Doht.

Chapter 1: Understanding the Transition

The day you leave rehab is a milestone, a moment that represents hope, freedom, and a fresh start. But it also carries a weight that many aren't prepared for—the realization that life outside the walls of rehab can be just as challenging, if not more so, than the time spent inside. While rehab gave you the structure and support to heal in a controlled environment, the real world is unpredictable. For some, leaving rehab feels like being thrown into the deep end after only learning to float.

Rehab taught you the basics: how to manage cravings, understand triggers, and navigate emotions without numbing yourself with substances. But those lessons are just the beginning. The transition to sober living marks a new chapter in your recovery, one that requires even more vigilance, dedication, and self-awareness. It's easy to feel overwhelmed. The safety net of rehab is gone, and now, it's up to you to build the support system you need to stay sober.

You might feel a mix of emotions: relief that rehab is over, fear of what lies ahead, and maybe even doubt about your ability to make it. These emotions are normal. Leaving the structure of rehab means stepping into a world where things aren't as predictable, where triggers can pop up without warning, and where you're now responsible for applying everything you've learned. But in this transition, there's also an incredible opportunity—to not just survive, but to begin truly living again.

In rehab, your days were probably structured with group sessions, therapy sessions, and routines that were all geared toward one goal:

staying sober. As you move into sober living, it's important to understand that this structure doesn't disappear just because you're no longer in treatment. If anything, creating and maintaining structure is one of the most critical tools you'll need moving forward. Routine can be your lifeline when cravings hit or when life starts to feel overwhelming. It provides a sense of control and stability, something that might feel elusive as you step out into a world that may seem chaotic and unpredictable.

One of the most important parts of your transition is recognizing that your recovery isn't over—far from it. It's easy to fall into the trap of thinking that completing rehab is the finish line, but in reality, it's just the first lap in a much longer race. Recovery is a lifelong process, and the skills you learned in rehab are the foundation you'll continue to build upon. As you transition into sober living, you'll be faced with new challenges that didn't exist within the protective bubble of rehab. Out in the world, you'll encounter people, places, and situations that could potentially trigger old behaviors and cravings. This is why it's essential to stay vigilant and aware. Just because you've made it through rehab doesn't mean you won't face moments of temptation. In fact, those moments might feel more frequent and intense now that you're re-entering your normal life.

But here's the truth: you're not the same person who went into rehab. You're stronger now. You've learned how to identify triggers and cope with them. You've built a toolkit of coping strategies—everything from deep breathing and mindfulness to calling a sponsor or attending meetings. These tools aren't just things you learned; they're now essential parts of your daily life. The trick is using them before you feel overwhelmed.

In sober living, your success will largely depend on how well you can create an environment that supports your recovery. It's about more than just avoiding old friends or places associated with your addiction; it's about surrounding yourself with people and habits that align with your new lifestyle. This might mean finding new hobbies, creating a morning routine, or even learning how to navigate social situations without feeling like you're missing out. At first, it might feel like you're walking a tightrope, balancing the need to engage with the world while protecting your sobriety. But over time, with practice, that balancing act becomes second nature.

One of the hardest parts of transitioning from rehab is dealing with the emotional waves that come with it. You might experience moments of intense joy—feeling proud of how far you've come and hopeful about the future. But there will also be moments of fear, sadness, or even anger. It's important to remember that these emotions are part of the process. For a long time, substances may have dulled or numbed your feelings, but now you're facing them head-on, raw and unfiltered. This is both a blessing and a challenge. The emotions you experience will guide your healing, but only if you allow yourself to feel them without judgment.

As you face these emotional highs and lows, don't forget to give yourself grace. Recovery is not a straight line; there will be setbacks and tough days. The key is to keep moving forward, even if it feels like you're taking baby steps. Each day that you choose not to drink or use is a victory, even when it doesn't feel like it. One of the most powerful things you can do in this phase is to practice self-compassion. Instead of beating yourself up for struggling, remind yourself that recovery is hard work, and you're doing your best. Treat yourself with the same kindness you would offer a close friend going through a tough time.

Another crucial element in your transition is community. In rehab, you were likely surrounded by others who were on the same journey. Sober living can feel lonelier, but it doesn't have to be. Building a support system is one of the most essential things you can do during this time. Recovery is not something you do in isolation; it thrives in connection with others who understand the path you're walking. Whether it's through a sober living home, 12-step meetings, or support groups, having people who know what you're going through can make all the difference.

These are the people you can lean on when you're feeling vulnerable, and they can hold you accountable when the temptation to slip back into old habits arises.

It might feel awkward at first to open up to others about your struggles, especially if you've spent a lot of your life hiding your addiction or feelings of shame. But vulnerability is the gateway to healing. When you share your experiences with others who've been there, you not only relieve some of the burden you've been carrying, but you also remind yourself that you're not alone. Addiction thrives in isolation, but recovery grows in community. This is why it's so important to stay connected to your support network, even if it feels uncomfortable at first.

One thing to keep in mind as you move forward is the importance of being intentional about who you allow into your life. Not everyone will support your sobriety, and that's okay. It's essential to set boundaries with people who may not be conducive to your recovery. This could mean distancing yourself from old friends who are still using or avoiding places that are too triggering. It might also mean having difficult conversations with family members or loved ones about your needs in recovery. Remember, it's okay to prioritize your well-being above all else. Sobriety is your foundation now, and anything that threatens that foundation needs to be reassessed.

At the same time, you'll likely find that there are people who surprise you with their support. You might reconnect with family or friends who lost touch with you during your addiction, or you may meet new people who encourage and motivate you in ways you never expected. Recovery opens the door to new possibilities and relationships that are based on trust, honesty, and mutual respect. This is one of the gifts of sobriety—you start to build real, meaningful connections that aren't clouded by the haze of addiction.

As you continue to transition from rehab into sober living, it's important to think about the bigger picture. What kind of life do you want to create now that substances are no longer in control? In many ways, this period is a chance for reinvention. You have the opportunity to rediscover who you are without drugs or alcohol defining your choices. This might involve exploring new interests or rekindling old passions that you lost touch with during your addiction. It could mean going back to school, finding a job that fulfills you, or simply taking the time to figure out what brings you joy and peace.

One of the most profound changes that happens in recovery is the shift from merely surviving to truly living. In addiction, life becomes about getting through the day, finding the next fix, or escaping painful emotions. But in recovery, you have the chance to embrace life fully, to be present in each moment without the fog of substances. It won't always be easy, and there will be times when you miss the numbness that addiction provided. But over time, as you learn to sit with your emotions and experience life as it is, you'll find that the highs are much higher and the lows are more manageable than they ever were in addiction.

It's important to remember that recovery is not just about staying sober; it's about building a life that makes sobriety worth it. This is where the concept of self-care becomes vital. You've already done the hardest part—choosing to live without substances. Now, it's about taking care of yourself in ways that nurture your body, mind, and spirit. This might mean adopting healthier habits like exercise, eating well, or practicing meditation. It could mean engaging in therapy to work through the underlying issues that contributed to your addiction in the first place. Or it might be as simple as giving yourself permission to rest and recover without constantly feeling like you have to do more.

Another aspect of building a life in recovery is learning to set goals. In addiction, long-term planning often takes a backseat to the immediate need for relief. But now that you're sober, you can start thinking about the future in a new way. What are your dreams? What do you want to achieve? Setting small, achievable goals can give you a sense of purpose and direction as you navigate this new phase of life. These goals don't have to be grand or ambitious at first—just something that keeps you moving forward. Over time, as you gain more confidence in your sobriety, you'll find that your goals start to expand, and with them, your belief in what's possible for your life.

The truth is, the transition from rehab to sober living is one of the most challenging parts of recovery, but it's also one of the most rewarding. It's the time when you take the lessons you've learned and start applying them to real life, building a foundation that can support you for years to come. It's not about being perfect; it's about being persistent. Every day you choose not to use is a victory, and each of those victories adds up over time. The more you commit to your recovery, the more you'll find that life in sobriety offers a richness and depth that addiction never could.

As you move forward, remember that it's okay to ask for help when you need it. Recovery is not a solo journey, and there will be times when you need support, whether it's from a sponsor, a therapist, or a friend in recovery. Lean on your community when things get tough, and don't be afraid to admit when you're struggling. Vulnerability is not a weakness—it's a sign of strength and courage. And in recovery, it's one of the most powerful tools you have.

This is the beginning of a new chapter in your life, one that is filled with possibility and hope. The road ahead won't always be easy, but you've already proven that you have the strength to overcome the hardest part. Now, it's about taking things one day at a time, trusting the process, and believing in your ability to build a life that is not only sober but full of meaning and purpose. You might still have moments where doubt creeps in, where the thought of going back to your old life feels like an escape from the overwhelming emotions and challenges of recovery. But every time you resist that temptation, you are not just choosing sobriety—you are choosing yourself. You're choosing your future, your potential, and everything you deserve that addiction tried to take from you. The decision to stay sober isn't just about avoiding the bad; it's about opening yourself up to all the good that is yet to come.

In the early days of sober living, you may find yourself questioning whether you're really capable of lasting change. Old fears and insecurities can resurface when you least expect them, and it's easy to wonder whether you'll always feel this vulnerable. But the truth is, vulnerability is part of being human. Learning how to sit with discomfort, how to face challenges without numbing yourself, is one of the greatest skills you'll ever develop. Over time, that vulnerability transforms into strength. Each day that you wake up and choose to keep going, you're proving to yourself that you are stronger than your addiction.

You may also find that people in your life don't fully understand what you're going through. Some may think that because you've completed rehab, the hard part is over. They may not realize that the fight for sobriety continues every day, long after you've left treatment. It's important to have patience—not only with yourself but with those around you. You can't expect everyone to understand the complexities of recovery, especially if they've never experienced addiction firsthand. But what you can do is communicate your needs clearly. Let the people who care about you know how they can support you, whether it's attending meetings with you, helping you stay accountable, or simply being there to listen when you're having a tough day.

As you build your new life in sober living, it's crucial to embrace the concept of progress over perfection. You're not going to get everything right all the time, and that's okay. Recovery isn't about doing things perfectly; it's about learning, growing, and becoming a better version of yourself with each passing day. You're going to have setbacks, and there will be days when the weight of it all feels unbearable. But those moments don't define you. What defines you is how you respond to them—whether you allow a mistake or a tough day to derail your progress, or whether you pick yourself back up and keep moving forward.

There will also be days when the progress feels slow, where you might wonder if you're really getting anywhere. But recovery is a journey, not a destination. Each small step adds up over time, even if you don't see the results immediately. Some days, success might look like attending a meeting or resisting a craving. Other days, it might simply mean getting out of bed and doing your best to face the day. Each of these moments matters. Each choice you make to stay sober strengthens the foundation you're building for a healthier, happier life.

As you continue to move forward, it's important to acknowledge the progress you've made. Take time to reflect on how far you've come since the days when addiction controlled your life. Celebrate the victories, no matter how small they might seem. Whether it's a week, a month, or a year of sobriety, these milestones are worth recognizing. They are tangible proof that you are capable of change, that you are capable of living a life free from substances. You've already proven your strength by making it this far, and now it's about sustaining that strength, one day at a time.

One of the most powerful aspects of recovery is the realization that you are not the person you were in your addiction. Addiction may have shaped parts of your past, but it doesn't define who you are today. You have the power to rewrite your story, to create a new narrative for your life that is centered around healing, growth, and self-discovery. This journey will continue to evolve as you learn more about yourself and what it means to live a life of purpose. In sobriety, you have the freedom to explore new paths, to build relationships that are based on trust and authenticity, and to pursue goals that align with the person you are becoming.

As the days turn into weeks, and the weeks into months, you'll begin to notice a shift. The cravings that once seemed unbearable will become more manageable. The emotions that once felt overwhelming will begin to soften, and you'll find new ways to cope with them. You'll discover parts of yourself that you had forgotten in the haze of addiction—passions, dreams, and strengths that were always there, waiting for you to uncover them. Sobriety will bring new challenges, but it will also bring new opportunities, new joys, and new possibilities that you never thought possible.

There will come a time when you'll look back at the person you were when you first left rehab, and you'll hardly recognize them. The transformation that happens in recovery is profound. It's not just about staying away from substances; it's about becoming the best version of yourself. You'll begin to trust yourself again, to believe in your own strength and resilience. And as that trust grows, so too will your confidence in your ability to navigate life without relying on substances.

Ultimately, the transition from rehab to sober living is about reclaiming your life. It's about taking back the control that addiction stole from you and using it to build something meaningful. It's about proving to yourself that you are capable of living a life that is full of hope, purpose, and possibility. The road ahead won't always be easy, but you've already shown that you have the strength to keep moving forward. Each day in recovery is a gift, an opportunity to continue the journey of healing, growth, and self-discovery.

So as you step into this new phase of your life, remember that you are not alone. You have the tools, the support, and the strength to make it through whatever challenges lie ahead. Recovery is not about being perfect; it's about showing up for yourself every day, no matter how hard it gets. And in doing so, you're not just surviving—you're thriving. You're creating a life that is not only sober but filled with the kind of joy, love, and fulfillment that addiction could never provide. Keep going. You're worth it.

Chapter 2: Establishing Daily Routines and Creating Structure in Recovery

One of the biggest challenges after leaving rehab is the sudden shift from a highly structured environment to one where you are responsible for building your own routine. In rehab, every moment is accounted for—from morning check-ins and therapy sessions to meals and evening reflection. But once you step into sober living, that structure is no longer imposed on you, and it's up to you to create a rhythm that supports your sobriety. It can feel liberating at first, but without a plan in place, the days can become overwhelming. This is where the power of daily routines comes in.

Having a daily routine provides stability during a time when everything else might feel uncertain. It gives you a sense of purpose and direction, allowing you to focus on your recovery without being weighed down by decisions about how to spend your time. It's not about being rigid or filling every moment with productivity; it's about giving yourself a framework that supports your healing and growth. Establishing a routine might feel like a small step, but it's one of the most effective ways to safeguard your sobriety and rebuild your life with intention.

The first step in creating this structure is designing a morning routine that sets the tone for your day. In addiction, mornings might have been filled with dread or chaos, but now you have the chance to start each day with purpose. The goal is to wake up with a clear mind and a positive attitude, ready to face whatever challenges lie ahead. A consistent morning routine can help ground you, especially on days when recovery feels hard. It doesn't have to be elaborate—what matters is that it's intentional.

Consider beginning your day with a moment of mindfulness or meditation. Even just five minutes of deep breathing or quiet reflection can make a difference in how you approach the rest of your day. Some people find comfort in starting their day with prayer or reading a passage from spiritual or recovery literature. Others prefer journaling to set their intentions or acknowledge their feelings. Whatever method works for you, the key is to take a moment to center yourself before jumping into the day's demands.

After your moment of reflection, moving your body is a powerful way to boost your mood and energy. Whether it's a quick walk, some light stretching, or a full workout, incorporating physical activity into your morning routine helps reduce stress and clears your mind. Exercise not only improves physical health but also releases endorphins, which are natural mood boosters. It can help manage cravings, reduce anxiety, and give you a sense of accomplishment early in the day. And it doesn't have to be intense—a gentle yoga session or a walk in the park can be just as effective in getting you grounded and focused.

As your morning routine sets the foundation, the rest of your day can be guided by structure and intention. One of the biggest pitfalls in early recovery is too much free time. Without a plan, idle moments can lead to restlessness, which can trigger thoughts of using. This is why creating a schedule is so important. It helps you stay productive and ensures that recovery remains your top priority.

Start by anchoring your schedule with recovery activities. These might include attending 12-step meetings, therapy sessions, or checking in with your sponsor. Recovery doesn't stop when you leave rehab; it's something you continue to work on daily. Having set times for these activities ensures that you stay engaged with your program and receive the support you need. Beyond recovery-specific activities, filling your day with meaningful tasks—whether it's work, volunteering, or simply cleaning your living space—helps maintain focus and purpose.

Balancing work and recovery can be tricky, especially if you're re-entering the workforce after rehab. It's important to pace yourself. If you're able, start with part-time work or a flexible schedule that allows you to attend meetings and take care of yourself. The goal isn't to overfill your days but to maintain a balance that supports both your financial and emotional well-being. If you're not working yet, consider dedicating time each day to looking for employment, developing new skills, or finding ways to give back to the community. Volunteering is a great way to reconnect with others and give your days a sense of purpose, while also contributing to your healing process.

Taking care of your body is just as important as managing your time. Physical health is often neglected in addiction, and recovery is an opportunity to start fresh. Incorporating healthy eating habits and regular exercise into your routine can have a huge impact on your overall well-being. Staying active is particularly important because it not only keeps your body healthy but also provides a healthy outlet for stress. You don't need to become a fitness enthusiast overnight—simple activities like walking, swimming, or biking can be enough to keep your body moving and your mind clear. The key is consistency. Finding an activity you enjoy will make it easier to stick to a routine, and over time, you'll start to feel the physical and emotional benefits.

Beyond physical health, emotional and mental self-care are critical components of your daily routine. Recovery can stir up a lot of emotions—grief, shame, anxiety, and fear among them. These emotions are normal, but without the crutch of substances, they can feel overwhelming at times. This is why it's important to find healthy ways to process your feelings and manage emotional stress. Developing emotional self-care practices can help you navigate those intense feelings without turning to old coping mechanisms.

One of the most effective tools for emotional self-care in recovery is journaling. Writing down your thoughts and feelings can be a way to process emotions that feel too big to handle internally. It provides a safe space to explore your fears, frustrations, and victories. Journaling also allows you to track your progress over time. Some days may feel harder than others, but when you look back at where you started, you'll see the growth that might not have been obvious in the moment. Journaling in the morning or before bed can become part of your routine, a way to check in with yourself and acknowledge where you are emotionally.

In addition to journaling, mindfulness and meditation can help you stay present and grounded. These practices don't require hours of commitment—just a few minutes of mindful breathing or sitting quietly with your thoughts can make a big difference. The goal of mindfulness isn't to eliminate difficult emotions but to observe them without judgment. This practice can help you respond to stress in healthier ways, rather than reacting impulsively. It can also be helpful when cravings or triggers arise, allowing you to create space between the urge to use and the decision to stay sober.

Incorporating creative outlets into your routine is another way to support your emotional health. Whether it's painting, writing poetry, playing music, or cooking, engaging in activities that bring you joy and satisfaction can help alleviate stress and keep your mind engaged in positive ways. Creative expression allows you to process emotions in ways that words alone can't always capture. It also gives you a sense of accomplishment and pride, helping to rebuild your self-esteem, which may have been eroded during active addiction.

As you establish your daily routines, it's important to set realistic goals for yourself. Early in recovery, it's tempting to want to fix everything all at once—to rebuild relationships, get a job, and achieve stability as quickly as possible. But recovery is a marathon, not a sprint. It's important to pace yourself and avoid setting expectations that are too high or unrealistic. Instead, focus on small, achievable goals each day.

This could be something as simple as making it to a meeting, cleaning a part of your living space, or completing a task at work. Setting and meeting these smaller goals will help you build confidence and create momentum over time.

Accountability plays a big role in sticking to your routine. One way to stay accountable is by sharing your daily goals with a sponsor, a therapist, or a trusted friend. Having someone to check in with regularly can help keep you on track and offer encouragement when things get tough. It's also helpful to use recovery tools, like apps or journals, that allow you to track your progress and reflect on your journey. The act of writing down your goals and reviewing them at the end of each day can give you a sense of accomplishment, even on days when it feels like you didn't get much done. Recovery is not about perfection, but progress, and every step forward counts.

As the day winds down, creating an evening routine is just as important as starting the day with intention. The transition from day to night can bring its own set of challenges. For many people in recovery, the evenings can be particularly difficult, as they might have been times when you turned to substances in the past. Developing a calming evening routine helps reduce stress and gives you time to reflect on your day in a positive way.

Winding down with a quiet activity, such as reading, listening to music, or taking a warm bath, can help signal to your body and mind that it's time to rest. Avoiding stimulating activities, like scrolling through social media or watching TV late into the night, can help you get better sleep and wake up feeling refreshed. If you're finding it difficult to sleep, incorporating mindfulness or breathing exercises before bed can help quiet a racing mind and make it easier to relax.

A nightly reflection practice can be a powerful part of your evening routine. Take a few moments to review your day—what went well, what challenged you, and what you're grateful for. Acknowledge your efforts and remind yourself that you're making progress, even if the day didn't go perfectly. Gratitude is a simple yet profound practice that can shift your mindset from focusing on what's missing to appreciating what you have. Ending the day with a moment of gratitude, whether by writing it down or reflecting silently, can help set a positive tone for the next day.

It's also helpful to end your day with a check-in, either with yourself or with a sponsor, partner, or trusted friend. This check-in can be as simple as reviewing your goals for the day or discussing any challenges you faced. Having someone to talk to can provide you with encouragement and accountability, helping you stay connected to your recovery. On the days when you're feeling strong, this check-in can reinforce your progress, and on the days when you're struggling, it provides an opportunity to ask for help and support.

Over time, these routines will become second nature, and the structure you create for yourself will provide a sense of stability and purpose. Recovery isn't about following a rigid schedule, but about creating habits that support your healing. Some days will feel easier than others, and that's okay. What matters is that you keep showing up for yourself, even on the hard days.

As you continue to build a daily routine that works for you, remember that this process takes time. Be patient with yourself as you adjust to life in sober living. The habits and routines you develop now will lay the foundation for long-term sobriety and personal growth. And as you move through this journey, remember that each day is an opportunity to practice self-care, stay connected to your recovery, and create the life you deserve.

By establishing a routine that supports your mental, physical, and emotional well-being, you're not just staying sober—you're creating a life of purpose and fulfillment. The daily choices you make, no matter how small, will add up over time, helping you build the strength and resilience needed to thrive in recovery. And in doing so, you're giving yourself the greatest gift of all: the opportunity to live a life free from addiction, where you can truly be present for yourself and those you love.

As you settle into your new routines, you may begin to notice subtle but significant changes in how you approach each day. There will be a growing sense of control over your time and energy, a newfound ability to make deliberate choices that prioritize your well-being. In addiction, life often felt chaotic, dictated by urges and impulses that pulled you in unpredictable directions. Now, with structure guiding your recovery, you're reclaiming that control. And with it, comes a sense of freedom—a freedom that allows you to engage fully with life, on your own terms.

However, it's important to acknowledge that routines alone won't solve everything. There will still be moments of difficulty, moments when cravings surface, when the weight of the past feels too heavy, or when life's challenges seem overwhelming. These moments are inevitable in recovery, but your routine provides a safety net—a series of positive habits that can help ground you when things get tough. When you're faced with temptation, stress, or emotional pain, the structure you've built around yourself can serve as a reminder of the progress you've made and the tools you have at your disposal.

In these difficult moments, it's crucial to lean on the supports you've put in place. Whether it's reaching out to a sponsor, attending a meeting, or simply taking time to meditate and breathe through the stress, your routine can help guide you through the storm. The routines you've established are not just about filling your days; they are about creating a foundation of stability, a framework within which you can respond to life's challenges with resilience and clarity.

One of the most valuable aspects of recovery is learning to navigate these challenges without returning to old coping mechanisms. It's about discovering that you have the capacity to face discomfort, uncertainty, and fear without numbing yourself. And as you continue to show up for yourself day after day, you will begin to realize just how strong you are. Recovery teaches you that you are capable of change—that even in the face of adversity, you can make choices that align with your values, your goals, and your sobriety.

Over time, the routines you've established will become the bedrock of your new life. They will help you maintain focus on your recovery, even as the initial intensity of post-rehab life begins to settle. As you grow more comfortable in your sober living environment, these routines will evolve, adapting to your changing needs and goals. What remains constant, however, is the importance of staying connected to your recovery—of recognizing that sobriety is not a destination, but a journey that requires continuous effort, reflection, and commitment.

As you move forward, it's important to celebrate the small victories along the way. Recovery is made up of these daily wins—moments when you chose to prioritize your well-being, moments when you leaned on your support network instead of isolating, moments when you resisted the urge to use. These victories may seem small in the moment, but they are the building blocks of lasting recovery. Each time you choose to stick to your routine, each time you show up for a meeting or complete a goal, you are reinforcing your commitment to yourself and to your sobriety.

In addition to celebrating your own progress, it's equally important to stay connected to the recovery community. Surrounding yourself with others who understand the journey you're on can provide invaluable support and encouragement. Whether it's through meetings, support groups, or sober living companions, being part of a community reminds you that you're not alone in this process. The shared experiences, wisdom, and strength of others can help bolster your own resolve when the road feels long or uncertain.

One of the most profound aspects of recovery is the opportunity to give back—to offer your own strength and experience to others who are still struggling. In time, you may find that you become a source of support for others, whether through sponsorship, volunteering, or simply offering a listening ear to someone in need. Helping others in their recovery journey not only reinforces your own sobriety but also gives you a sense of purpose and connection that goes beyond the individual. You become part of something bigger—a network of people working together toward healing and wholeness.

As this chapter draws to a close, remember that establishing daily routines is about more than just organizing your time. It's about creating a life that is meaningful, fulfilling, and aligned with your values. It's about finding balance between self-care, responsibility, and joy. And most importantly, it's about recognizing that recovery is not just about staying sober—it's about living a life that is worth staying sober for.

The routines you develop now will serve as the foundation for that life. They will help you navigate the ups and downs of recovery, providing you with stability and clarity even in the most challenging times. As you continue to build these habits, be gentle with yourself.

There will be days when things don't go as planned, when old patterns resurface, or when the weight of life feels heavy. But each day is a new opportunity to recommit to your recovery, to start fresh, and to choose the path of healing.

In the end, recovery is not about perfection—it's about progress. It's about taking each day as it comes, learning from the past without being defined by it, and moving forward with hope, courage, and resilience. The routines you establish today will become the stepping stones to the life you are building—a life that is free from the chaos of addiction, full of possibility, and grounded in the strength of your recovery journey.

As you move into the next phase of your sober living experience, remember that you are not defined by your past but by the choices you make today. And each choice, no matter how small, is a step toward a future filled with health, happiness, and the peace that comes from living in alignment with your true self. Keep moving forward, one day at a time, trusting that the routines you've built will carry you toward the life you've always deserved.

Recovery, like life, will ebb and flow. There will be seasons of strength, where the routines you've cultivated seem effortless, and others where it feels as though each day is a battle to maintain your footing.

In those harder times, it's crucial to remember that growth is not linear. Setbacks and struggles are part of the journey, but they don't erase the progress you've made.

You might find that your emotions surprise you in unexpected ways. Feelings you've pushed aside or numbed for years may begin to surface now that you're no longer using substances to dull them. This is a normal and necessary part of the healing process. Early in sobriety, it's common to feel a heightened sense of vulnerability. For many, this rawness can be disorienting. After years of living in survival mode, suddenly being present in your life—without the crutch of substances—can feel both liberating and terrifying.

It's during these times of emotional intensity that your routines and support systems will serve you the most. When feelings like shame, regret, or anger surface, your first instinct may be to run from them. But it's important to remember that emotions, even the uncomfortable ones, are not your enemy. They are signals, telling you where healing is needed. Instead of turning away from these feelings, try to meet them with compassion. Recognize that they are part of your recovery process, part of the story you're rewriting.

Sobriety grants you the opportunity to face life head-on, and that means experiencing both the highs and the lows. You might find yourself mourning the time lost to addiction, relationships that were damaged, or the person you used to be. Grief is an inherent part of recovery, but it's also an invitation to let go of what no longer serves you. As you grieve, remember that you are not defined by your past. You are allowed to feel sadness for what was, while still holding hope for what can be. This balance of grief and hope is at the core of healing.

In these moments of emotional difficulty, it's helpful to remind yourself of your "why"—the reasons you chose recovery. Maybe it's for your health, for your family, or simply because you deserve better. Reconnecting with your motivation can help ground you when the road ahead feels uncertain. And as you continue to face these challenges, your ability to navigate them without substances will strengthen, reinforcing your confidence and resilience.

As your emotional world becomes richer and more complex in sobriety, you may also experience the joy that comes with rediscovering parts of yourself that were buried by addiction. Maybe it's a creative passion, a long-lost hobby, or a connection with loved ones that begins to blossom again. These rediscoveries are like small pieces of yourself returning home, reminding you of who you truly are beneath the layers of pain and addiction. They are evidence that recovery is not just about staying sober—it's about reclaiming your life in all its fullness.

Another key element in your journey is forgiveness, both for yourself and others. For many, this is one of the most difficult aspects of recovery. The wreckage caused by addiction can leave deep scars—on relationships, on your self-esteem, and on your sense of worth. But as you continue to do the work of recovery, it's essential to remember that healing requires forgiveness. You can't change the past, but you can take responsibility for your actions moving forward. Self-forgiveness is not about excusing past behavior but about acknowledging your humanity and your right to grow from your mistakes.

Forgiving others is equally complex. You may have people in your life who hurt you deeply during your addiction, or whose actions contributed to your pain. Forgiveness in this context doesn't mean condoning their behavior—it means releasing the hold that resentment and anger have over you. Holding on to bitterness only keeps you stuck in the past. Letting go allows you to move forward with a lighter heart, free from the chains of old wounds.

As you deepen your recovery, you'll also begin to understand that this journey is not just about getting clean—it's about healing on every level: emotionally, mentally, physically, and spiritually. Addiction is a disease that affects the whole person, and so too must recovery address the whole self. There's no one-size-fits-all solution for healing, but by staying connected to your routines, your support systems, and your personal growth, you are laying the groundwork for lasting change.

You'll continue to face moments of doubt, frustration, and even fear. But with each day that you choose sobriety, you are building a foundation of strength that will carry you through these moments. Your recovery is not fragile—it is a powerful testament to your resilience, to your ability to rise again, no matter how many times you may have fallen in the past. Each day sober is a victory, a step closer to the life you deserve.

There will be times when you'll need to adjust your routines, adapt to new challenges, or seek additional support. Recovery is an ever-evolving process, one that requires flexibility and patience. What works for you today may need to be adjusted as you grow and change. The important thing is to stay connected to your goals and to be willing to ask for help when needed. Reaching out for support is a sign of strength, not weakness.

As you move forward, take time to acknowledge the milestones, both big and small. Whether it's celebrating a month sober, mending a relationship, or simply waking up and choosing recovery for another day, these moments are worth honoring. Recovery is a series of choices, and each choice you make in favor of your sobriety is a step toward the life you are building—a life of authenticity, freedom, and fulfillment.

In the end, your recovery is a reflection of your deepest strength, your ability to overcome the obstacles that once seemed insurmountable. The routines you've established, the relationships you've nurtured, and the healing you've embraced all contribute to the foundation of the new life you're creating. There will still be challenges ahead, but you now have the tools, the support, and the inner strength to face them with courage and clarity.

This journey is uniquely yours, and it's one that you're walking with intention, bravery, and grace. As you continue down this path, remember that you are worthy of the life you're creating. Sobriety is not just about living without substances—it's about living with purpose, with joy, and with the knowledge that you have the power to shape your future. One day at a time, you are transforming your life, and that is something to be deeply proud of.

As you move forward in your recovery journey, it's important to cultivate a sense of patience with yourself. It's natural to want everything to fall into place quickly, to feel as though you've mastered sobriety and left the chaos of addiction far behind. But the truth is, recovery is a lifelong process, one that requires ongoing care and attention. There will be moments when progress feels slow or setbacks occur, and it's in these moments that you must remind yourself that healing takes time.

You didn't get to this place overnight, and the wounds caused by addiction will not heal overnight either. There's a profound beauty in the slow, steady progress you make each day, even when it feels imperceptible. Some days, success may simply look like staying sober through a difficult situation. Other days, it might be about reconnecting with your passions, finding joy in simple moments, or deepening your relationships with loved ones. Every step you take toward recovery is significant, no matter how small it may seem.

During this time, one of the greatest gifts you can give yourself is the practice of self-compassion. It's easy to be hard on yourself, to dwell on the mistakes of the past, or to feel frustrated when you don't meet your own expectations. But recovery isn't about being perfect—it's about being human. It's about learning to forgive yourself for your imperfections and recognizing that every day is a chance to begin again. Be gentle with yourself. Treat yourself with the same kindness and understanding that you would offer to a friend in recovery.

Self-compassion is a powerful tool, especially in moments of self-doubt or when facing old patterns of thinking. When you find yourself slipping into negative self-talk or harsh criticism, take a step back and ask yourself: Would I speak to someone I care about this way? The answer is almost always no. The same kindness you extend to others is the kindness you deserve as well. Your recovery is an act of love for yourself, and that love should include moments of grace and patience as you navigate the ups and downs of this journey.

Another critical aspect of your ongoing recovery is maintaining a connection to your purpose. Sobriety opens up the space for you to explore what truly matters to you—what gives your life meaning and fulfillment. For some, this might be rekindling relationships that were damaged by addiction. For others, it might be discovering new passions, hobbies, or even career paths that align with their values. Whatever it is that lights you up inside, let that be your guiding star in recovery.

As you continue to reflect on your purpose, it's important to remember that it can evolve. What drives you today might shift as you grow and change in sobriety, and that's okay. The key is to stay curious about what brings you joy and fulfillment, and to be open to the new possibilities that sobriety brings. Life in recovery isn't just about avoiding relapse—it's about building a life that excites you, a life that feels worth living. When you have a strong sense of purpose, it can serve as a powerful motivator to stay on the path of sobriety, even in challenging times.

Purpose also extends beyond your own personal fulfillment. Many people in recovery find that helping others becomes an integral part of their journey. Whether through volunteering, mentoring, or simply being there for a friend in need, giving back can provide a sense of connection and meaning that is incredibly rewarding. The act of helping others reminds you that you are part of something larger than yourself, part of a community of people working toward healing and growth.

As you settle into sober living, you may find that your relationships begin to shift as well. Some relationships will deepen, while others may naturally fall away. This is a normal part of the recovery process. Addiction often strains relationships, and not all connections can be mended. Some people from your past may not be able to support your new life in sobriety, and it's important to acknowledge this with compassion. Letting go of toxic or unsupportive relationships is not a sign of failure—it's a necessary part of protecting your recovery and prioritizing your well-being.

At the same time, recovery presents the opportunity to build new, healthier relationships. You may find yourself gravitating toward people who share your values and support your journey. Surrounding yourself with those who encourage your growth and understand the challenges of recovery is crucial. Sober living environments often provide a space where these kinds of relationships can flourish, as you're surrounded by others who are also working toward sobriety. Lean into these connections, as they can provide invaluable support during difficult times.

As you continue to rebuild your life, don't forget the importance of gratitude. Gratitude has the power to shift your perspective, helping you focus on what you have, rather than what you've lost. In recovery, it's easy to get caught up in what's missing—the time lost to addiction, the relationships that couldn't be repaired, the mistakes you've made. But when you practice gratitude, you begin to see the abundance in your life. You begin to recognize the beauty in the small moments—the quiet mornings, the laughter with friends, the clarity of a sober mind.

Gratitude doesn't mean ignoring the challenges of recovery. It means holding space for both the struggles and the blessings, and choosing to focus on the latter. Each day sober is a gift, an opportunity to continue growing and healing. Even on the hardest days, there is always something to be grateful for, whether it's the support of a friend, the progress you've made, or simply the fact that you've chosen to stay sober for another day.

As you reflect on the journey ahead, remember that recovery is not a race. There is no finish line, no point at which you've "arrived" and can stop working on yourself. Recovery is a continuous process of learning, growing, and evolving. Some days will be easier than others, and that's okay. What matters is that you continue to show up for yourself, even on the hard days. Keep choosing sobriety, keep choosing healing, and keep believing in your own resilience.

In the end, the life you are building in recovery is not just a life without substances—it's a life full of possibility, connection, and meaning. It's a life where you can fully experience joy, love, and peace. The routines, the support systems, the inner work you're doing—these are all tools that will help you continue to move forward, one day at a time. Trust in the process, trust in yourself, and know that you are capable of creating a life that is truly worth living.

You've already come so far. Let that be a reminder of your strength and your ability to overcome whatever challenges lie ahead. Keep moving forward, and know that each step you take in recovery is a step toward a brighter, more fulfilling future.

Chapter 3: Building a Sustainable Sober Lifestyle

As you navigate the journey of recovery, you'll find that the transition from rehab to sober living isn't just about maintaining sobriety; it's about building a fulfilling life that supports your newfound freedom. This chapter focuses on creating a sustainable sober lifestyle, one that embraces growth, joy, and resilience.

To thrive in sobriety, it's essential to set long-term goals that inspire you. Goals provide a sense of direction and purpose, helping you envision the life you desire. Reflect on what truly matters to you. What do you want to achieve in your career? How do you envision your relationships? What personal interests or passions do you want to explore? Writing down these aspirations is a powerful first step, allowing you to articulate your dreams and break them down into actionable steps. For instance, if your goal is to advance in your career, consider what skills or qualifications you need and how you can obtain them. You might enroll in a course, seek mentorship, or network with others in your field. Setting both short-term and long-term objectives creates a roadmap that guides you through the complexities of sober living.

As you set goals, remember that building healthy routines is equally crucial. Routines create structure, which can be particularly beneficial in the early stages of sober living. When your days are filled with predictable activities, you're less likely to feel overwhelmed or bored—two feelings that can lead to cravings. Start your day with intentional practices that ground you. This might include meditation, journaling, or light exercise. These rituals set a positive tone for your day and keep your mind focused on your recovery.

Engaging in hobbies you love is another vital aspect of creating a routine. Explore interests that bring you joy—whether it's painting, gardening, cooking, or writing. Reconnecting with these passions can be incredibly therapeutic and remind you of who you are beyond your addiction. As you establish your daily routine, be sure to incorporate time for relaxation and self-care. Life in sober living can be busy, and it's essential to recharge your batteries to maintain your well-being.

Managing triggers and stressors is an inevitable part of building a sustainable sober lifestyle. Triggers can come in many forms—certain places, people, or emotions that elicit cravings or temptations to use substances. Being aware of your triggers is the first step in managing them effectively. Keep a journal to document situations that lead to cravings and identify patterns. This self-awareness empowers you to develop strategies for coping when faced with these challenges. When you encounter a triggering situation, have a plan in place to respond constructively. This could involve reaching out to a support person, practicing deep-breathing exercises, or engaging in a distracting activity. It's about finding what works for you and ensuring you have a toolbox of coping mechanisms at your disposal.

Stress management is another critical component of maintaining sobriety. Life can be unpredictable, and stress can lead to feelings of overwhelm, making it easier to revert to old coping mechanisms. Incorporating stress-reduction techniques into your routine—such as mindfulness meditation, yoga, or regular exercise—can significantly improve your emotional resilience. These practices help regulate your emotions and provide a healthy outlet for releasing tension.

As you embrace your sober lifestyle, engaging in a supportive community becomes increasingly important. Recovery can often feel isolating, but surrounding yourself with others who understand your journey can provide a sense of belonging and encouragement. Seek out support groups or recovery programs in your area, where you can share your experiences and learn from others. Building new friendships that align with your sober lifestyle is equally vital. These connections will help reinforce your commitment to recovery and provide a network of support during challenging times. Consider also volunteering or getting involved in community activities. Contributing your time and skills can foster a sense of purpose and remind you of the strength you've cultivated in your recovery journey.

Celebrating milestones is a crucial aspect of building a sustainable sober lifestyle. Each step you take in your recovery deserves recognition, whether it's a month of sobriety, a new job, or simply overcoming a challenging day. Celebrating your progress reinforces your achievements and reminds you of how far you've come. Establish personal rituals for celebrating milestones—treat yourself to something special, share your achievements with friends and family, or reflect on your journey through journaling. Acknowledging the challenges you've faced and the strength it took to overcome them is essential for maintaining motivation in your recovery.

As you move forward in this journey, remember that building a sustainable sober lifestyle is an ongoing process. It requires commitment, intention, and a willingness to embrace change. Each day presents an opportunity to live intentionally, to grow, and to embrace the beauty of life in sobriety. You have the power to shape your future and create a life that nourishes your spirit and fosters your recovery.

In this chapter, we've explored the importance of setting long-term goals, establishing healthy routines, managing triggers, engaging in community, and celebrating milestones. These elements are vital in creating a fulfilling and sustainable sober lifestyle. As you continue on your journey, embrace the challenges and triumphs that come your way. Each experience contributes to your growth and serves as a reminder of your strength and resilience.

You are not defined by your past; instead, you are the author of your story. The next pages are waiting to be written, filled with new adventures, discoveries, and the promise of a bright future. As you embrace this journey, understand that every day offers a blank slate. Each morning brings the opportunity to rewrite your narrative, to choose hope over despair, and to envision a life steeped in possibility. This realization can be both exhilarating and daunting, yet it is a powerful reminder of the agency you have in your recovery journey.

To fully embrace this chapter of your life, it's crucial to cultivate a mindset of growth. A growth mindset encourages you to view challenges as opportunities for development rather than insurmountable obstacles. Instead of fearing failure, welcome it as a natural part of the learning process. When setbacks occur—and they will—allow yourself to reflect without judgment. Ask yourself what you can learn from the experience. This mindset shift can transform how you approach difficulties, turning them into stepping stones rather than stumbling blocks.

Building resilience also requires nurturing a sense of gratitude. While it's easy to focus on what you've lost or what's gone wrong, take time to recognize the blessings in your life, however small they may seem. Keeping a gratitude journal can be an effective practice—jot down three things you're thankful for each day. This simple act can shift your focus away from negativity, fostering a sense of abundance and appreciation for the present moment. Gratitude can serve as a powerful antidote to the struggles of recovery, helping you maintain perspective and find joy in everyday life.

As you continue writing your story, remember to involve others in your journey. Sharing your experiences, both the triumphs and the challenges, can deepen your connections with those around you. Vulnerability fosters intimacy, allowing others to see your authentic self. When you open up about your struggles, you may find that others relate to your experiences, creating a supportive bond that can bolster your recovery. Whether through support groups, friendships, or family, building a community of understanding individuals can provide you with strength and encouragement.

Incorporating regular self-reflection into your routine can also enhance your journey of growth and resilience. Set aside time each week to evaluate your progress, revisit your goals, and assess your emotional state. This dedicated time for self-assessment allows you to stay attuned to your needs and desires. Ask yourself questions like: What am I proud of this week? What challenges did I face, and how did I respond? What do I need to change or improve moving forward? Engaging in this practice can help you identify patterns, adjust your approach, and ensure that you're actively working toward the life you envision.

Furthermore, don't shy away from seeking professional guidance when needed. Therapy or counseling can be incredibly beneficial as you navigate the complexities of recovery. A trained professional can help you develop coping strategies, work through unresolved issues, and offer insights that can lead to profound personal growth. Seeking help is not a sign of weakness; rather, it is a courageous step toward healing and self-discovery.

As you write your story, you will encounter numerous plot twists—some unexpected, some challenging, and others beautifully surprising. Embrace these twists as part of your unique journey. The richness of your experiences, both good and bad, will shape the person you are becoming. Celebrate the small victories along the way, as they contribute to the larger narrative of your life. Remember, it's not just about the destination; it's about the journey itself and the lessons learned along the way.

As this chapter closes, reflect on the incredible strength you possess. You are capable of creating a life that is vibrant, meaningful, and fulfilling. The foundation you have built in recovery provides you with the tools necessary to face whatever comes next. Embrace change, cultivate resilience, and continue writing your story with intention and purpose. Each decision you make, each relationship you nurture, and each goal you pursue adds depth to your narrative.

Ultimately, the path to a sustainable sober lifestyle is not a straight line but a dynamic process of growth and self-discovery. You hold the pen; your life is yours to create. Let the pages ahead be filled with love, laughter, and a commitment to living fully in the present. The future is bright, and it's yours for the taking.

Embracing this new chapter requires not only setting the foundation for a fulfilling life but also cultivating a mindset that embraces continual growth and transformation. To truly thrive in sobriety, you must foster a sense of purpose in everything you do. This sense of purpose acts as a guiding light, helping you navigate the ups and downs of recovery with resilience and determination.

To establish a sense of purpose, reflect on the values that matter most to you. What do you stand for? What brings you joy and fulfillment? Consider how these values can shape your daily decisions and interactions. Aligning your actions with your core values not only enhances your sense of self but also strengthens your commitment to recovery. For instance, if family is a significant value for you, prioritize spending quality time with loved ones. Engaging in activities that resonate with your values creates a meaningful framework for your life, allowing you to stay focused and motivated.

Another essential aspect of a sustainable sober lifestyle is developing a proactive approach to mental health. Recovery is not solely about abstaining from substances; it's about nurturing your emotional well-being. Recognize the importance of mental health in your overall recovery journey and seek ways to prioritize it. Engage in practices that promote emotional resilience, such as therapy, mindfulness, or journaling. Surround yourself with positivity—read uplifting books, listen to inspiring podcasts, and engage with content that nurtures your spirit.

As you strive to maintain your sobriety, remember that it's perfectly normal to encounter moments of vulnerability and uncertainty. These feelings don't signify failure; instead, they are part of the human experience. It's essential to develop self-compassion during these moments. Speak to yourself with kindness, as you would to a friend facing similar struggles. Acknowledge your feelings without judgment, and remind yourself that it's okay to have difficult days. Practicing self-compassion fosters resilience and helps you approach challenges with a sense of understanding rather than shame.

To further fortify your sobriety, it's beneficial to create a personal mantra or affirmation that resonates with you. This mantra can serve as a reminder of your strength and purpose during challenging times. For example, you might adopt a phrase like "I am worthy of love and happiness" or "I embrace each day as an opportunity for growth." Repeating this affirmation daily can reinforce a positive self-image and cultivate a mindset that is aligned with your goals.

In addition to personal affirmations, consider establishing rituals that honor your journey. These rituals can be as simple as lighting a candle during meditation, taking a walk in nature to clear your mind, or practicing gratitude before bed. Rituals provide a sense of stability and intention, reminding you to stay present and mindful in your recovery. They can become anchors in your daily life, helping you to center yourself amidst the chaos that may arise.

As you continue to build a sustainable sober lifestyle, it's vital to remain adaptable. Life is inherently unpredictable, and the ability to adjust your plans and expectations can significantly impact your recovery. Embrace flexibility as a strength rather than a weakness. When faced with unexpected challenges, allow yourself to pivot and explore alternative solutions. This adaptability not only fosters resilience but also helps you to remain open to new experiences and opportunities.

Your journey toward a sustainable sober lifestyle also involves cultivating healthy boundaries. Boundaries are essential in maintaining your sobriety and protecting your well-being. Assess your relationships and identify those that support your recovery versus those that may pose a risk. Communicate your needs clearly and assertively, and don't hesitate to distance yourself from individuals or situations that threaten your progress. Establishing boundaries is a powerful act of self-care, allowing you to prioritize your recovery and create a safe environment for growth.

Engaging in self-care is equally crucial as you navigate your journey. Self-care isn't a luxury; it's a necessity for maintaining your mental, emotional, and physical well-being. Create a self-care plan that includes activities that rejuvenate and inspire you. This might involve regular exercise, practicing mindfulness, spending time with loved ones, or indulging in creative outlets. Prioritize self-care as a non-negotiable part of your routine, understanding that it lays the groundwork for your long-term recovery.

As you reflect on the journey you've undertaken, take time to acknowledge the lessons you've learned along the way. Each experience—whether joyful or painful—has contributed to your growth. Consider keeping a journal to document your thoughts, feelings, and insights. This practice not only provides an outlet for self-expression but also allows you to track your progress over time. Revisit your entries periodically to remind yourself of how far you've come and to reflect on the growth you've experienced.

In the spirit of continual growth, seek out opportunities for learning and development. Whether through formal education, workshops, or self-directed study, expanding your knowledge can provide new perspectives and tools to navigate the challenges of sober living. Lifelong learning fosters a sense of curiosity and engagement with the world around you, reinforcing your commitment to self-improvement.

As you approach the closing of this chapter, remember that building a sustainable sober lifestyle is a journey, not a destination. Embrace the ebb and flow of your experiences, and trust that you have the strength to face whatever comes your way. The road may be winding, but with each step, you are shaping a life that reflects your true self—one that is rich in purpose, connection, and joy.

You have the power to write a narrative that inspires not only yourself but also others who may walk a similar path. Your story can serve as a beacon of hope, illuminating the way for those still grappling with the darkness of addiction. As you move forward, carry this knowledge with you: You are not alone, and your journey matters.

Let your story be one of resilience, growth, and unwavering commitment to a brighter tomorrow. Embrace the challenges, celebrate the victories, and continue to create a life that aligns with your true self. The pages ahead are unwritten, waiting for you to fill them with your truth.

Chapter 4: The Journey of Renewal

As you continue on this path of recovery, it becomes increasingly important to embrace the concept of renewal. Just as nature undergoes cycles of change, so too does your journey. Recovery is not a linear path; it's a dynamic process filled with opportunities for growth, learning, and transformation. This chapter invites you to reflect on where you've been, acknowledge where you are now, and envision the possibilities that lie ahead.

Renewal begins with introspection. Take the time to assess your journey so far. What lessons have you learned? What strengths have emerged in you that you didn't know existed? Reflecting on your experiences allows you to appreciate the progress you've made and reinforces your commitment to your recovery. Consider journaling your thoughts, creating a timeline of your journey, or simply engaging in quiet contemplation. This process of reflection not only deepens your understanding of yourself but also cultivates gratitude for the resilience that has brought you to this moment.

To facilitate this introspection, set aside a dedicated time each week for self-reflection. Find a quiet space where you can think without distractions. Bring a journal or a notebook and ask yourself guiding questions such as: What have been my biggest challenges during recovery, and how have I overcome them? What moments have brought me joy and fulfillment? In what ways have I changed since I started this journey? How do I envision my life in the next year, five years, or even ten years? Writing down your thoughts can help clarify your feelings and provide insight into the patterns in your life.

As you look back, it's equally important to envision your future. Setting intentions for what you want to achieve in your recovery can provide clarity and motivation. These intentions can be broad or specific, ranging from personal goals like pursuing a new career, nurturing relationships, or enhancing your well-being. Write down your intentions, and don't hesitate to revisit and revise them as you grow. This practice keeps you focused on the future you are creating while grounding you in the present.

One powerful exercise is to create a vision board. Gather images, quotes, and symbols that resonate with your aspirations and place them on a board or a digital collage. This visual representation serves as a constant reminder of your intentions and the life you are working toward. Hang it somewhere you'll see daily, allowing it to inspire you as you navigate each day. The act of creating a vision board can itself be therapeutic, allowing you to engage creatively with your goals while fostering a sense of hope and excitement about the future.

The process of renewal also involves redefining your relationships. The people in your life significantly influence your recovery experience. Now is the time to nurture connections that uplift and inspire you while letting go of those that no longer serve your growth. Engage in honest conversations with friends and family about your journey, expressing your needs and boundaries. Establishing healthy communication lays the groundwork for stronger, more supportive relationships moving forward. It's important to remember that not everyone will understand your journey, and that's okay. Surround yourself with those who uplift you, share your goals, and encourage your progress.

Additionally, consider surrounding yourself with positive influences. Seek out recovery communities, support groups, or friendships with individuals who understand the challenges you face. These connections can provide a sense of belonging and remind you that you are not alone in your journey. Sharing your experiences and hearing the stories of others can foster a sense of unity and understanding, reinforcing the idea that recovery is a collective experience. For instance, if you find yourself at a support group meeting, share a bit of your story and listen to the journeys of others. Notice how their experiences reflect your own, and offer support and encouragement when you can. The bonds formed in these spaces can become vital components of your support network.

In this phase of renewal, it's also essential to cultivate self-care practices that resonate with you. Recovery requires energy, focus, and commitment, which can be challenging without a solid self-care routine. Explore various self-care techniques—such as physical activities, mindfulness practices, hobbies, or relaxation techniques—that nourish your body and spirit. Discover what replenishes your energy and brings you joy. Whether it's a daily walk in nature, a creative project, or simply taking time to unwind with a good book, prioritize these activities to sustain your well-being. You might find it helpful to develop a weekly self-care schedule that includes time dedicated to various activities. For example, set aside time on Mondays for exercise, Wednesdays for creative pursuits, and Sundays for quiet reflection. Treat these appointments with the same importance you would a work meeting or a doctor's appointment. This commitment to self-care sends a message to yourself that you are worthy of love and attention.

As you embrace renewal, be mindful of the need for flexibility. Life is unpredictable, and your recovery journey will inevitably present challenges and surprises. Cultivating resilience means adapting to change while remaining committed to your intentions. Develop coping strategies that empower you to navigate stress and uncertainty. This might include grounding techniques, deep breathing exercises, or reaching out to your support network during tough times. Embracing flexibility allows you to move through life's ups and downs with grace, knowing that setbacks are a natural part of growth.

Think of resilience as a muscle; the more you work at it, the stronger it becomes. You can enhance this muscle through small, everyday practices. For instance, when faced with a challenge, take a moment to pause and breathe. Rather than reacting impulsively, allow yourself the space to respond thoughtfully. This practice can prevent you from reverting to old coping mechanisms and can help you find healthier alternatives. In addition, incorporate mindfulness practices into your routine. Whether through meditation, yoga, or simple breathing exercises, these practices ground you in the present moment and help manage anxiety and stress. You might begin with just five minutes each day, gradually increasing as you become more comfortable with the practice. The benefits of mindfulness extend beyond the immediate moment, contributing to long-term emotional regulation and resilience.

Remember, renewal is not about erasing your past; it's about integrating your experiences into a fuller understanding of yourself. Each challenge, each moment of struggle, has contributed to the person you are today. Embrace the idea that your past does not define you; rather, it serves as a backdrop against which your story of resilience and strength unfolds. Allow yourself to feel the full spectrum of emotions that accompany this journey, from joy to sadness, as they are all integral to your growth. The journey of renewal encourages you to embrace change while honoring your authentic self. As you work through these emotions, practice self-compassion. Remind yourself that it's okay to feel what you're feeling and that every emotion is valid. Cultivating self-compassion can soften the harsh inner critic that often emerges during challenging times, allowing you to treat yourself with the same kindness you would offer a friend.

In this chapter of renewal, set aside time to celebrate milestones in your recovery. Acknowledging your progress, no matter how small, reinforces your commitment to this journey. Whether it's a month of sobriety, a successful completion of a personal goal, or a moment of clarity in your understanding of yourself, take the time to honor these achievements. Celebrations can take many forms—gathering with friends, treating yourself to something special, or simply reflecting on your journey with gratitude. These moments serve as reminders of your capability and the bright future that awaits you.

Consider creating a personal tradition for celebrating milestones. This might be as simple as treating yourself to a favorite meal or as elaborate as planning a gathering with friends who have supported you throughout your journey. The key is to make the celebration meaningful to you. Create a ritual that resonates with your experiences and honors the hard work you've put into your recovery. This could also include writing a letter to yourself to read at significant milestones, outlining your growth, achievements, and aspirations. Keeping this letter can serve as a motivational tool to reflect on during challenging moments, reminding you of how far you've come.

As you move forward, keep in mind that renewal is an ongoing process. Embrace the idea that each day offers an opportunity for growth, reflection, and transformation. Approach life with an open heart and a curious mind, ready to explore new experiences and learn from each moment. Your journey of renewal is uniquely yours, and it holds the potential to inspire not only your life but also the lives of those around you.

Renewal is not merely a phase; it is a way of life. Embracing a mindset of renewal allows you to view challenges as opportunities for learning rather than obstacles to your progress. This shift in perspective is powerful. It opens you to the possibilities that exist in every situation. When faced with a setback, ask yourself: What can I learn from this? How can this experience contribute to my growth? By adopting this mindset, you not only foster resilience but also cultivate a deeper understanding of yourself and your journey.

As you journey deeper into renewal, it's essential to recognize the role of community in your process. Humans are inherently social beings, and the connections we forge significantly impact our well-being. Building a support network of individuals who understand the complexities of recovery can provide a crucial foundation for your growth. Whether it's through friends, family, support groups, or mentors, these relationships can offer encouragement, perspective, and a sense of belonging.

Consider reaching out to those who inspire you or those who have walked similar paths. Share your experiences and invite them to share theirs in return. These interactions can foster deeper connections and remind you that you are not alone in your journey. The power of community lies in its ability to create a safe space where you can express your feelings, share your triumphs, and find comfort during difficult times. Seek out local recovery groups, workshops, or online communities where you can connect with others on a similar journey. Engaging in discussions and sharing stories can provide valuable insights and reinforce your commitment to your recovery.

Engaging in community activities can also enhance your sense of purpose and fulfillment. Look for opportunities to give back, whether through volunteering, mentoring others in recovery, or simply being there for someone who needs support. Acts of service can create a sense of connection and purpose, reminding you that your journey holds value not just for yourself but for those around you. By contributing to the well-being of others, you reinforce the belief that change is possible and that your story can inspire others to seek their path to recovery.

Additionally, focus on creating rituals that symbolize renewal and growth in your life. These can be small daily practices or larger annual traditions that mark your progress and celebrate your achievements. Consider establishing a "renewal day" where you reflect on your journey, set new intentions, and take time for self-care. Use this day to engage in activities that inspire you, whether it's exploring nature, creating art, or simply spending time in solitude. These rituals can become anchors in your recovery, helping you stay grounded and focused on your goals.

As part of your renewal journey, you might find it beneficial to explore new interests and passions. Recovery offers a unique opportunity to rediscover or even discover aspects of yourself that may have been buried during your struggles. Try to immerse yourself in new experiences, whether that's taking up a new hobby, learning a new skill, or pursuing an interest you've always wanted to explore. This exploration can reignite your curiosity and enthusiasm for life, reminding you that there is so much more to experience beyond your past.

Embracing creativity can also be a powerful tool for renewal. Artistic expression—whether through painting, writing, music, or any other medium—can provide an outlet for emotions and a way to process your journey. Allow yourself the freedom to create without judgment. Whether you create a piece of art that reflects your emotions, write poetry about your experiences, or simply journal your thoughts, these acts of creativity can foster healing and self-discovery. If you're unsure where to start, consider setting aside time each week for creative expression. Treat it as a sacred space where you can explore your thoughts and feelings without pressure.

Moreover, your journey of renewal might also lead you to explore holistic practices that promote well-being. Incorporating mindfulness, meditation, or yoga into your routine can enhance your mental clarity, emotional stability, and physical health. These practices encourage you to stay present in the moment, reduce anxiety, and cultivate self-awareness. You might begin with just a few minutes each day and gradually increase your practice as you become more comfortable. Resources like guided meditation apps or local classes can provide structure and support as you navigate these new practices.

As you embrace these various aspects of renewal, remember to be gentle with yourself. Change can be daunting, and growth often comes with discomfort. Allow yourself the grace to feel whatever arises during this process. Recognize that setbacks are not failures but rather opportunities to learn and grow. Practice self-compassion, acknowledging that you are doing your best in a challenging journey. This mindset shift can be liberating, allowing you to approach your recovery with a sense of curiosity rather than judgment.

Additionally, surrounding yourself with positive affirmations can significantly impact your mindset. Create a list of affirmations that resonate with you, focusing on your strengths, your journey, and your potential. Repeat these affirmations daily to reinforce your belief in yourself and your ability to overcome challenges. These powerful statements can serve as reminders of your resilience and your commitment to renewal. You might even consider posting them in visible places around your home, turning your environment into a sanctuary of encouragement.

Another critical aspect of your journey is recognizing the importance of patience. Recovery and renewal take time, and progress is often gradual. Embrace the idea that every small step counts, no matter how insignificant it may seem. Celebrate these small victories, for they pave the way for larger achievements. Patience allows you to cultivate a deeper understanding of yourself and your needs, fostering growth in ways you may not immediately recognize.

As you navigate this journey of renewal, be open to change and the unexpected. Life has a way of presenting challenges that can lead to profound growth. Embrace the uncertainty with an open heart, knowing that each experience contributes to your personal evolution. This openness allows you to adapt to new circumstances, learn from experiences, and grow into the person you are meant to be.

Finally, as you reflect on your journey, remember to embrace joy. Recovery is not just about overcoming challenges; it's also about discovering happiness and fulfillment in the present moment. Seek out moments of joy, no matter how small they may be. Whether it's enjoying a warm cup of coffee, spending time with loved ones, or simply witnessing a beautiful sunset, allow yourself to soak in these experiences fully. Cultivating joy can provide a counterbalance to the struggles of recovery, reminding you that life is a tapestry of both challenges and beauty.

In conclusion, the journey of renewal is ongoing, filled with opportunities for growth, connection, and self-discovery. Embrace this phase with an open heart, knowing that you are forging a path toward a brighter future. Allow your experiences, both past and present, to guide you as you continue to write your story. Each day is a blank page, waiting for you to fill it with your dreams, hopes, and aspirations. Embrace the beauty of your journey, the resilience you've shown, and the transformative power of renewal.

As you embark on this new chapter of your life, the process of renewal also invites you to redefine your identity. For many individuals in recovery, the labels of the past can feel overwhelming or limiting. It's crucial to recognize that while your past experiences are part of your story, they do not define who you are today or who you can become. This chapter focuses on the transformative journey of self-discovery, inviting you to explore the depths of your identity beyond the shadows of addiction.

Begin by reflecting on the person you want to become. Consider the values that resonate with you and the qualities you admire in others. What aspects of yourself do you want to nurture and develop? Crafting a vision of your future self can be a powerful motivator in your recovery journey. Write down the characteristics and attributes you aspire to embody. This could include being resilient, compassionate, creative, or adventurous. By articulating these traits, you create a roadmap for your personal development, allowing you to take tangible steps toward becoming the person you envision.

A significant part of redefining your identity involves letting go of limiting beliefs. Many individuals carry negative self-perceptions formed during their struggles with addiction. These beliefs can manifest as feelings of unworthiness, shame, or doubt. Challenge these narratives by consciously acknowledging your strengths and accomplishments. Keep a journal where you document your achievements, no matter how small they may seem. Reflect on the challenges you've overcome and the lessons you've learned along the way. This practice can help shift your mindset from one of self-doubt to one of empowerment, enabling you to embrace a more positive self-image.

Additionally, consider surrounding yourself with positive influences. The people you spend time with can significantly impact your self-perception. Seek out individuals who uplift you and encourage your growth. Engage in conversations that inspire you and challenge you to think differently. As you build connections with others who are also committed to their growth, you create a supportive environment that reinforces your journey of renewal. Let go of relationships that drain your energy or hinder your progress, and instead focus on nurturing connections that align with your values and aspirations.

As you redefine your identity, explore the concept of self-compassion. This means treating yourself with the same kindness and understanding that you would offer a dear friend. Recovery is a complex journey, and it's essential to acknowledge that setbacks may occur. Instead of harshly criticizing yourself during challenging times, practice self-compassion by offering gentle encouragement and support. Remind yourself that you are human, and it's okay to stumble along the way. Embracing self-compassion allows you to cultivate resilience and fosters a healthier relationship with yourself.

In this exploration of self-discovery, consider the role of mindfulness. Mindfulness practices encourage you to be present in the moment and cultivate awareness of your thoughts and feelings without judgment. Engaging in mindfulness can help you recognize patterns in your behavior and thought processes, allowing you to make conscious choices that align with your desired identity. Start with simple practices, such as focused breathing or body scans, to ground yourself in the present. Over time, you can incorporate mindfulness into daily activities, enhancing your awareness and promoting emotional well-being.

Alongside mindfulness, developing a daily gratitude practice can have a profound impact on your perspective. Gratitude shifts your focus from what is lacking in your life to what is abundant. Each day, take a moment to reflect on the things you are grateful for, whether big or small. Consider keeping a gratitude journal where you jot down three things each day that bring you joy or appreciation. This practice fosters positivity and helps you cultivate a sense of fulfillment, reminding you of the blessings in your life as you navigate your journey of renewal.

As you delve deeper into self-discovery, remember to embrace your passions. Rediscovering the activities that bring you joy can be a powerful way to reconnect with your authentic self. Make a list of hobbies or interests you've always wanted to explore or rekindle. Whether it's painting, dancing, hiking, or writing, allow yourself the freedom to engage in these activities without the pressure of expectations. Embrace the idea that these pursuits are not just pastimes but integral parts of your identity.

Furthermore, consider setting aside time for creative expression. Engaging in artistic activities can provide an outlet for emotions and allow you to explore your thoughts in a different way. Try to immerse yourself in the process of creation rather than focusing solely on the outcome. Whether it's picking up a paintbrush, writing poetry, or playing an instrument, let your creativity flow freely. This practice can serve as a powerful reminder of your ability to create beauty and meaning in your life, reinforcing your sense of self.

As you continue on this path, it's essential to recognize the importance of goal-setting in your journey of self-discovery. Setting personal goals gives you a sense of direction and purpose, allowing you to align your actions with your evolving identity. Reflect on what you want to achieve in different areas of your life—career, relationships, personal development, and health. Write down specific, measurable goals and break them into actionable steps. As you work toward these objectives, celebrate your progress along the way. Acknowledging your achievements reinforces your sense of agency and empowers you to continue moving forward.

Moreover, consider the impact of self-reflection in your journey. Set aside regular time to reflect on your experiences, emotions, and thoughts. This could involve journaling, meditating, or simply sitting in quiet contemplation. Use this time to check in with yourself, assess your progress, and evaluate whether your actions align with your values and aspirations. Self-reflection cultivates self-awareness and enables you to make adjustments when necessary, ensuring that you remain true to your evolving identity.

As you redefine your identity and embrace your journey of renewal, remember to practice patience with yourself. Change is a gradual process, and growth takes time. Celebrate the small victories and recognize that setbacks are part of the journey. Be open to the unfolding of your story, allowing it to develop naturally as you navigate the complexities of life in sobriety. Each experience, whether joyous or challenging, contributes to the richness of your journey and shapes the person you are becoming.

In conclusion, the path to self-discovery is a dynamic and transformative process. Embrace the opportunity to redefine your identity, explore your passions, and cultivate a deeper understanding of yourself. Allow your experiences to guide you, and trust that you are capable of creating a fulfilling and meaningful life. Remember that you are the author of your own story, and as you turn each page, you have the power to shape your narrative. The journey of renewal is a beautiful exploration of who you are and who you can become, and it is filled with endless possibilities for growth and fulfillment.

Chapter 5: Cultivating Resilience in Recovery

As you navigate the complex landscape of sobriety, one of the most vital attributes you can develop is resilience. Resilience is the ability to bounce back from adversity, adapt to challenges, and maintain a positive outlook even in difficult circumstances. This chapter explores the multifaceted nature of resilience, providing you with tools and insights to cultivate this essential trait in your recovery journey.

Resilience is not an innate quality; rather, it is a skill that can be developed through intentional practice and a shift in mindset. Begin by understanding that setbacks are a natural part of life, especially in recovery. It's crucial to reframe how you perceive challenges. Instead of viewing setbacks as failures, consider them opportunities for growth. Each obstacle you encounter can teach you something valuable about yourself and your capacity to overcome adversity. This shift in perspective empowers you to approach difficulties with a sense of curiosity rather than fear.

A key aspect of building resilience is fostering a growth mindset. This concept, popularized by psychologist Carol Dweck, emphasizes the belief that abilities and intelligence can be developed through effort and learning. Embrace the idea that you have the capacity to learn from your experiences and adapt your strategies as needed. When faced with challenges, ask yourself: What can I learn from this situation? How can I grow stronger because of it? By adopting a growth mindset, you empower yourself to face setbacks with determination and an open heart.

Another critical element in cultivating resilience is building a strong support network. Surround yourself with individuals who uplift and encourage you, especially during difficult times. This network may include friends, family, mentors, or support group members who understand your journey. Sharing your struggles with others can provide a sense of relief and validation, reminding you that you are not alone in your experiences. Consider attending support group meetings regularly to connect with others who are also navigating the challenges of recovery. These relationships can become a lifeline, offering guidance, inspiration, and understanding.

In addition to external support, nurturing your internal resources is equally important. This involves developing self-awareness and emotional intelligence, which enable you to recognize your feelings and respond to them constructively. Practice tuning into your emotions without judgment. When you experience frustration or disappointment, take a moment to acknowledge those feelings. Instead of suppressing them, allow yourself to feel and process these emotions. Journaling can be a helpful tool in this regard; writing about your experiences can provide clarity and insight, helping you identify patterns and triggers in your emotional responses.

As you cultivate resilience, it's essential to establish healthy coping strategies. Life will inevitably present challenges, but having a toolbox of effective coping mechanisms can make all the difference in how you navigate those difficulties. Explore various coping strategies and identify which ones resonate with you. This could include mindfulness practices, such as deep breathing, meditation, or yoga, which help ground you in the present moment. Physical exercise is another powerful way to release stress and boost your mood. Find an activity you enjoy, whether it's running, dancing, or practicing martial arts, and make it a regular part of your routine.

Moreover, engaging in creative expression can be an incredible outlet for processing emotions and fostering resilience. Whether it's painting, writing, music, or any form of artistry, creative activities allow you to channel your feelings into something constructive. This form of expression not only provides relief but also helps you gain insight into your experiences, enhancing your emotional resilience over time.

Building a sense of purpose is another cornerstone of resilience. When you have a clear sense of purpose, you are better equipped to face challenges and stay motivated during difficult times. Reflect on what gives your life meaning—this could be your relationships, passions, career aspirations, or contributions to your community. Identify ways to integrate your sense of purpose into your daily life. Volunteering, for example, can provide a sense of fulfillment and connection, reinforcing the idea that your experiences have value and significance beyond yourself.

Additionally, practicing self-care is vital in your journey toward resilience. When life gets challenging, it can be easy to neglect your own needs, but prioritizing self-care is essential for maintaining your emotional and physical well-being. Establish a self-care routine that encompasses various aspects of your life, including nutrition, exercise, sleep, and relaxation. Make time for activities that bring you joy, whether it's reading a book, taking a nature walk, or enjoying a warm bath. By nurturing yourself, you create a solid foundation for resilience, allowing you to face life's challenges with strength and clarity.

As you continue to cultivate resilience, remember that it's okay to seek professional help if needed. Therapy or counseling can provide valuable support and tools for navigating difficult emotions and experiences. A trained professional can guide you in developing coping strategies tailored to your unique needs, empowering you to build resilience more effectively.

In this chapter, we've explored the importance of resilience in recovery and the various ways you can cultivate it. From shifting your mindset and building a support network to developing healthy coping strategies and nurturing your sense of purpose, each element plays a crucial role in fostering resilience. As you face the ups and downs of life, remember that resilience is not about avoiding challenges but rather about embracing them with courage and determination. You have the strength within you to rise above adversity, and as you do, you'll discover a deeper sense of self and a renewed appreciation for the beauty of life in sobriety.

As you continue your journey, remind yourself that resilience is a journey, not a destination. Each experience contributes to your growth, and with each step, you become more capable of navigating life's complexities. Trust in your ability to adapt and thrive, and embrace the possibilities that await you. You are building a life rich with purpose, joy, and resilience, and this chapter is just one of many in your ongoing story of recovery.

As you continue to strengthen your resilience, it's important to embrace the idea that resilience is not about avoiding discomfort but rather about how you respond to it. In recovery, discomfort can arise from many places—whether it's confronting difficult emotions, navigating social situations without the crutch of substances, or facing fears about the future. These moments of discomfort are inevitable, but they also present powerful opportunities for growth.

Learning to sit with discomfort, rather than trying to escape it, can be a transformative part of your journey. In the past, substances may have been your go-to way of coping with stress, fear, or uncertainty. Now, in recovery, the task is to cultivate new ways of handling these feelings.

One approach is to remind yourself that discomfort, like all emotions, is temporary. It will pass, even if it feels overwhelming in the moment. Practice grounding techniques, such as focusing on your breath, feeling your feet on the floor, or reminding yourself of something tangible in your environment. This mindfulness can create a buffer between your emotions and your reactions, allowing you to respond rather than react impulsively.

In fact, some of the most profound breakthroughs in recovery come from moments of discomfort. These are the moments when you are faced with the choice to either fall back into old habits or rise to meet the challenge in a new way. With time and practice, you will find that each time you choose resilience, each time you lean into the discomfort rather than avoid it, you grow stronger. You gain confidence in your ability to handle what life throws your way without resorting to substances.

Another crucial aspect of resilience is learning to embrace change. Recovery is all about transformation—of your habits, your relationships, your mindset, and even your identity. This level of change can feel overwhelming, especially when the future feels uncertain. However, viewing change as an opportunity rather than something to fear can help ease this transition. Instead of seeing recovery as the end of something, see it as the beginning of something entirely new.

One way to embrace change is to stay open to new experiences and perspectives. Recovery invites you to redefine what a meaningful life looks like for you. It's a chance to rediscover old passions, explore new hobbies, and surround yourself with people who support your growth. Being open to change means allowing yourself to evolve. You don't have to hold onto old versions of yourself just because they feel familiar. Give yourself permission to grow, to let go of the past, and to step into a new chapter of your life.

In addition to personal change, recovery often brings changes to your social landscape. The relationships you had before and during addiction may need to be redefined or, in some cases, released altogether. While this can be painful, it's important to remember that healthy relationships are those that support your sobriety and well-being. Surround yourself with people who encourage your growth and celebrate your recovery journey, rather than those who tempt you to return to old habits.

At the same time, be patient with yourself and others as you navigate these social shifts. Building new, healthy relationships takes time, but it's worth the effort. Consider joining recovery groups or engaging in sober activities where you can meet others who understand your experiences. These connections will not only offer you support but also help you build a community of people who are invested in your success.

As you work on rebuilding your social circle, remember that it's okay to feel lonely at times. Loneliness is a natural part of the recovery process, especially if you've had to distance yourself from people or places that were once central to your life. But loneliness doesn't have to be a negative experience. It can also be a time of self-reflection and growth. Use it as an opportunity to get to know yourself better and to cultivate the kind of inner strength that will serve you in the long run.

In addition to embracing change and managing discomfort, resilience in recovery also means maintaining hope. Hope is the light that guides you through the darker moments of your journey. It's the belief that, no matter how challenging the path may be, better days are ahead. Keeping hope alive can be difficult, especially when progress feels slow or setbacks occur, but hope is what sustains you when things get tough.

One way to nurture hope is to practice gratitude. Gratitude shifts your focus away from what's missing or what's difficult and redirects it toward what's positive in your life. Each day, make a conscious effort to recognize the things you are grateful for, whether it's a supportive friend, a peaceful moment in nature, or the simple fact that you are sober today. Gratitude doesn't ignore life's challenges, but it reminds you that there is always something to be thankful for, no matter how small.

You can also keep hope alive by setting intentions for the future. While it's important to take recovery one day at a time, having a vision for your future can provide a sense of purpose and direction. What kind of life do you want to create in your sobriety? What dreams have you put on hold that you are now ready to pursue? Allow yourself to dream again and to believe that a fulfilling, meaningful life is not only possible but within reach.

As you continue on this journey, there will undoubtedly be moments when your resilience is tested. There will be days when the weight of recovery feels heavy, when the old temptations resurface, or when life throws unexpected challenges your way. In those moments, remember everything you have already overcome. You have survived your darkest days, and you have emerged stronger for it. You have the tools, the support, and the inner strength to face whatever comes next.

Recovery is not a straight path, but rather a journey of ups and downs, twists and turns. There will be setbacks, but there will also be victories. The important thing is that you keep moving forward, one step at a time. Each day you choose sobriety, each time you face discomfort and embrace change, you are building a foundation for a life that is not only free from addiction but full of meaning, joy, and purpose.

In closing, remember that resilience is not about being perfect or never feeling weak. It's about rising every time you fall, continuing to believe in yourself, and trusting that you are capable of creating a life worth living. You have already come so far, and the best is yet to come. Hold on to that hope, keep nurturing your resilience, and know that every step forward brings you closer to the life you deserve.

With that in mind, as you continue this process of growth and transformation, stay open to the many possibilities that life in recovery has to offer. Each new day is a fresh start, a new opportunity to live with intention and purpose. And while the road may not always be easy, it will always be worth it. You have the strength, the courage, and the resilience to succeed.

Chapter 6: Facing Setbacks with Grace

Setbacks are a natural part of life, and in recovery, they are almost inevitable at some point. It's important to remember that setbacks don't define your journey, but rather how you respond to them does. In this chapter, we'll explore how to handle setbacks with grace, resilience, and the wisdom to learn from each experience.

One of the most difficult things about recovery is acknowledging that the path forward won't always be linear. There may be moments when old habits or temptations resurface, or when life throws challenges your way that feel overwhelming. Whether it's a lapse in sobriety or simply feeling emotionally stuck, these moments can feel discouraging. But they are also opportunities for growth and self-compassion.

The first step in facing a setback is to recognize it without judgment. We often feel shame or guilt when we experience a setback, as though it's a sign of personal failure. But recovery is a process, and setbacks are simply part of that process. Instead of condemning yourself for the setback, acknowledge it for what it is: a moment in your journey. It does not erase the progress you've made or your commitment to sobriety.

When a setback occurs, take a moment to reflect on what led to it. Was there a particular trigger, stressor, or emotional experience that made you vulnerable? Understanding the cause of the setback can help you develop strategies to prevent it from happening again in the future. This reflection should be done with kindness toward yourself, rather than self-criticism. Everyone faces challenges in recovery; what matters most is how you use those challenges to strengthen your resolve moving forward.

Another key to navigating setbacks is reaching out for support. When things go wrong, the instinct might be to retreat into isolation or keep the setback to yourself. But recovery thrives on connection, and sharing your experiences with others can help lift the burden of shame. Whether it's with a sponsor, a therapist, or a supportive friend, talking about what happened allows you to process the event and gain perspective.

Support systems are there to remind you that you're not alone. Other people in recovery understand what it's like to face setbacks, and they can offer guidance, encouragement, or simply a listening ear. There's no need to hide your struggles or pretend everything is okay when it isn't. Being honest about your setbacks is a sign of strength, not weakness.

Sometimes, setbacks can make you feel like you're starting from square one, but that's rarely the case. Even if you've experienced a lapse or a difficult period, you still carry with you all the lessons, tools, and growth from your journey so far. Recovery isn't about never making mistakes; it's about continually choosing to get back up after you fall.

In moments of setback, self-compassion becomes crucial. Often, our inner critic can be loud and unforgiving, telling us that we've failed or that we're not capable of recovery. But being harsh with yourself only deepens the wound. Instead, practice speaking to yourself with the same kindness you would offer to a friend in a similar situation. Remind yourself that you are human, that setbacks happen to everyone, and that you are still worthy of healing and growth.

Use setbacks as an opportunity to revisit your goals and recommit to your recovery plan. It can be helpful to reassess what's working and what isn't, adjusting your approach as needed. Perhaps you need to reengage with a support group, add more structure to your day, or focus more on your self-care practices. A setback can be a signal that something in your routine or strategy needs attention, and addressing it with a proactive mindset can help you move forward.

It's also important to celebrate your resilience. Even in the face of setbacks, you're still here, still working toward your sobriety, and that's something to be proud of. Recovery is about progress, not perfection, and each time you get back up after a setback, you're reinforcing your commitment to a better life. Every time you choose to keep going, you're proving your strength and dedication.

One of the most powerful lessons you can learn from setbacks is that they are not the end of your story. They are chapters in a much larger narrative of transformation and growth. The road to recovery isn't always smooth, but each obstacle you overcome adds to your resilience and your ability to face future challenges. In time, you'll find that setbacks don't have to derail your progress; they can be stepping stones to deeper self-awareness and renewed commitment.

Remember that setbacks can be a chance to reconnect with your purpose. Why did you start this journey in the first place? What is it that you're striving for in your life? Reconnecting with your deeper purpose can give you the strength to keep moving forward. When setbacks happen, use them as an opportunity to remind yourself of your "why." Whether it's to rebuild relationships, to achieve personal goals, or simply to live a healthier and more fulfilling life, that purpose will help reignite your motivation and guide you through difficult times.

In fact, setbacks can often strengthen your resolve. They offer you the chance to confront challenges head-on and emerge with a greater sense of clarity about what matters most. As you navigate the twists and turns of recovery, you'll become more attuned to your own needs and boundaries. Over time, you'll develop a stronger foundation that allows you to handle difficulties with more grace and confidence.

One way to remain connected to your purpose is to create a list of affirmations or reminders of why you've chosen the path of sobriety. This list can serve as a powerful touchstone during times when you feel overwhelmed by a setback. Writing down these reasons gives them tangible form, making them harder to ignore when you're faced with temptations or struggles. Keep the list somewhere visible, like on your phone, in your journal, or taped to your bathroom mirror, so it's accessible when you need encouragement the most.

In addition to reaffirming your purpose, reflect on the lessons that the setback has offered you. What have you learned about yourself? What vulnerabilities have been exposed, and how can you strengthen those areas moving forward? Every setback holds within it a seed of wisdom if you choose to approach it with an open mind. These lessons are invaluable and can guide you as you continue to grow in your recovery.

It's essential to stay patient with yourself throughout this process. Healing doesn't happen overnight, and setbacks don't erase your progress. When we talk about recovery being a journey, it means that there will be ups and downs, victories and losses, but through it all, you are moving forward. Even if it feels like two steps back, you're still in motion, and every effort you make to rise again counts.

Forgiving yourself for past missteps and allowing yourself the space to stumble is vital. True progress in recovery comes not from avoiding all mistakes but from learning how to recover from them with grace. Each setback gives you another opportunity to practice that grace—to be gentle with yourself, to understand your limitations, and to approach your healing process with compassion.

Surround yourself with a strong support network that will help lift you up when times get tough. Building relationships that reinforce your sobriety, whether through peer support groups, recovery communities, or friendships, can be a lifeline during difficult times. Reach out and let people know when you're struggling. Lean on your community; after all, recovery is not something that you have to do alone.

As you close this chapter, let the setbacks you've faced be reminders of your resilience. Every time you've gotten back up, every time you've recommitted to your path, you've proven that you have the strength to carry on. Embrace the lessons that come from these experiences and know that you are continuously moving toward a future filled with growth, healing, and self-discovery.

There will always be challenges in life, but how you respond to them will define the quality of your recovery. Setbacks are part of the process, not the end of the story. Continue to move forward, embrace each new lesson, and remember that every step, no matter how small, is progress.

In the end, recovery is not about avoiding all difficulties or becoming perfect. It's about learning how to handle life's inevitable challenges with grace, and with the understanding that each setback is an opportunity for renewal. Keep going, keep believing in yourself, and keep writing the story of your own healing—one filled with hope, resilience, and the courage to continue, no matter what comes your way.

Chapter 7: A New Beginning—Embracing Life Beyond Sober Living

As you stand at the threshold of a new chapter in your life, there's a feeling of both excitement and uncertainty. You've completed your time in sober living, a place where you learned to rebuild, re-center, and reclaim your life. Now, with the tools, support, and resilience you've cultivated, it's time to step fully into the world outside, to embrace the freedom that sobriety brings and navigate life with a renewed sense of purpose.

The journey to this point wasn't easy, and it's important to acknowledge how far you've come. There were moments when the path seemed impossible—when the weight of addiction felt too heavy to bear. But through sheer determination, the support of your community, and a willingness to heal, you've made it through. And now, as you leave behind the structure of sober living, you carry with you a deep well of inner strength, ready to face the world on your terms.

The end of sober living isn't the end of your recovery journey—it's a new beginning. The lessons you've learned during your time there will continue to guide you, but now you have the freedom to craft your life in ways that are meaningful to you. There's a sense of liberation that comes with this new phase, a chance to redefine who you are and what your life can become.

As you step forward, one of the most empowering things you can do is to trust yourself. For so long, addiction may have eroded your belief in your own abilities, but recovery has shown you what you're capable of. You've faced some of the darkest moments of your life and emerged stronger. Trust that this strength will continue to carry you through any challenges that come your way.

In this new chapter, it's crucial to remember that life in sobriety is not about perfection—it's about progress. There will still be ups and downs, moments of doubt, and unexpected obstacles. But each of these experiences will provide an opportunity for growth. Instead of seeing them as setbacks, view them as part of your evolution. The skills you've honed in sober living—such as managing triggers, building routines, and seeking support—will remain your allies in this new phase of life.

One of the most powerful aspects of life after sober living is the freedom to build the life you've always envisioned. For so long, addiction may have taken away your ability to dream, to set goals, or to believe in your own potential. Now, you have the chance to reclaim those dreams and make them a reality. Whether it's pursuing a career, rebuilding relationships, or simply finding joy in everyday moments, this is your time to explore what truly fulfills you.

It's also a time to continue building a strong support network. Just because you're leaving sober living doesn't mean you have to go through life's challenges alone. Stay connected with the people who've been part of your journey, whether through support groups, friendships, or mentors. Surround yourself with individuals who uplift and encourage you, who understand the challenges of recovery and celebrate your victories. Having a solid community can make all the difference as you transition into this next chapter.

Another key to long-term success is to maintain the routines and practices that helped you thrive in sober living. These routines provide structure and stability, which are essential as you adjust to life outside of the recovery environment. Whether it's maintaining a morning meditation practice, continuing with exercise, or dedicating time to hobbies that bring you joy, these daily rituals will help anchor you in your new life.

As you move forward, it's important to continue setting goals for yourself—both big and small. Recovery has taught you the importance of progress, and now is the time to keep that momentum going. Perhaps you want to advance in your career, travel to new places, or deepen your relationships. Whatever your aspirations, take the time to break them down into manageable steps. Celebrate each milestone along the way, and give yourself credit for the progress you make.

One of the most beautiful aspects of life beyond sober living is the opportunity to give back. The experiences you've had, the struggles you've overcome, and the wisdom you've gained can be a source of inspiration and guidance for others who are still in the early stages of recovery. Whether it's volunteering, mentoring, or simply sharing your story, your journey can provide hope to someone else who may be struggling. In giving back, you not only help others but also reinforce your own commitment to sobriety and personal growth.

As you reflect on your journey, remember that recovery is a lifelong process. It's not something that ends when you leave rehab or sober living—it's a continuous journey of learning, growing, and evolving. There will always be new challenges and new lessons to learn, but with each step, you become more resilient and more empowered to create the life you want.

You have already come so far, and the road ahead is full of possibility. Embrace it with open arms, knowing that you have everything you need to succeed. Trust in your own strength, lean on your support system, and keep moving forward with intention and purpose. Life beyond sober living is your opportunity to shine, to rediscover joy, and to live with authenticity and fulfillment.

This final chapter is not the end of your story—it's the beginning of a new, vibrant, and empowered life. The tools you've gained, the lessons you've learned, and the inner strength you've cultivated will continue to guide you as you write the next chapters of your life. Take pride in your journey, and know that no matter what lies ahead, you have the courage and resilience to face it with confidence.

About the Author

I was born on December 18, 1991, in Litchfield, Illinois. My mother, Tracy, worked hard to provide a stable life for me and my younger sister, born on November 16, 1993, despite facing challenges in her relationships. My mother's marriage to my sister's father ended due to his cocaine addiction, and her brief marriage to Will became toxic due to his abusive behavior. After that annulment, she dedicated herself to healing and stability.

High school brought new struggles; I battled weight issues and a sense of not fitting in. I turned to smoking weed and drinking, which led to a cycle of anger and bullying. By high school graduation, my drinking escalated, and I was sneaking vodka and using pills. This destructive lifestyle only worsened after school, driving me deeper into addiction.

After high school, I moved away and met my daughter's father, who initially helped me quit drugs, but my addiction resurfaced after I began working at a bar. This led to our separation and ultimately losing custody of my daughter as my drug use spiraled. I hit my lowest point when I was shooting meth and isolating myself. My family pressed charges for fraud, resulting in jail time, which unexpectedly forced me to reflect and begin regaining my sanity.

After jail, I returned to drugs, experimenting with fentanyl, which led to multiple overdoses and the tragic loss of my boyfriend in February 2020. I entered rehab but struggled to maintain sobriety, relapsing just before reaching six months in a sober living home. My life continued to spiral with homelessness and arrests, including a brief, dysfunctional marriage to a drug dealer.

Finally, I found hope with Matt, who shared my struggles. We endured addiction and homelessness together but eventually sought help. We entered treatment, and I moved into a sober living house while Matt stayed with a friend in recovery. My journey has been filled with pain and loss, but today, I stand in recovery, ready to embrace the future.